Groundhogs

Curious Kids Press

Please note:All Rights Reserved. No part of this publication may be reproduced in any form or by any means, including scanning, photocopying, or otherwise without prior written permission of the copyright holder. Copyright © 2014

Groundhogs

The Groundhog is a rodent. It is sometimes called, a woodchuck, a whistle-pig and a land-beaver. It is closely related to the marmot. The Groundhog is famous and has its very own day - Groundhog Day. This legend is celebrated each February 2nd to see how long it will be before Spring arrives. If the groundhog sees his shadow, 6 more weeks of winter will follow. Let's explore some more fun facts about this interesting rodent. Read on to dig into the cool world of the groundhog.

Where in the World?

Did you know these rodents can be found in many parts of the world? Groundhogs can be found in North America and are also common in the northeastern and central United States. These hairy critters will also live in Canada and as far north as Alaska.

The Habitat of the Groundhog

Did you know the groundhog likes to be around areas where woodlands meet open spaces? This can include fields, roads or streams. If you have tasty treats in your garden, you may find a groundhog there as well. They can quickly destroy gardens in the summer and early fall seasons.

The Body of a Groundhog

Did you know the groundhog is very low-to-the-ground? It has a stocky body and short legs. It can weigh up to 10 pounds (4.5 kilograms) and measure around 27 inches in length (68.5 centimeters). Its fur is a grizzled brown and it has darker brown to black feet. It also has small ears, large black eyes, a furry tail and a cute nose.

The Teeth of the Groundhog

Did you know this rodent has a distinct pattern of teeth? It has 4 large incisor teeth. These are used for biting off vegetation and also for gnawing through roots when tunneling. The groundhog's teeth keep growing; about 0.16 inches (0.4 centimeters) per-week. But because the groundhog is constantly wearing them down again, they never get too long.

The Feet of a Groundhog

Did you know the groundhog has sharp claws on its toes? Like all rodents in the marmot family, the groundhog has 4 clawed-toes on its front feet. On the back feet it has 5 clawed-toes. Along with its strong legs, these claws help it dig out long tunnels and to climb trees.

What a Groundhog Eats

Did you know the groundhog has been known to raid farmer's gardens? They love to eat beans, peas, herbs, strawberries and even flowers like pansies and impatiens. If there are no gardens to raid, the groundhog will dine on vegetation, nuts, seeds, grubs, grasshoppers, insects, snails and other small animals.

The Ground Hog's Special Ability

Did you know the groundhog is a true hibernator? This means it sleeps the entire winter away. The groundhog will go into its den from October through to February. It seals the sleeping chamber with dirt, then curls into a ball and falls asleep. It will live off of its body fat until springtime.

The Groundhog as Prey

Did you know many animals prey on the groundhog? Because this rodent spends most of its time on the ground, it is hunted by many predators. Wolves, cougars, coyotes, foxes, bobcats, bears, eagles and even some dogs all hunt the groundhog. Baby groundhogs often fall prey to snakes that sneak into their burrow.

Groundhog Talk

Did you know the groundhog has many ways of communicating? When alarmed or scared, the groundhog will make a high-pitched whistle. This is done to warn the rest of the groundhogs of the danger. It will also make a low barking sound. This is done by grinding its teeth together. This roden will also "puff-up" when it is scared. This makes it appear larger.

The Groundhog Burrow

Did you know Groundhogs are excellent burrowers? They use their burrows for sleeping, rearing young and hibernating. The average groundhog can move up to 5,500 pounds ((2,500 kilograms) of dirt when it is making a new burrow. The burrow can have 2 to 5 entrances and measure around 46 feet long (14 metres).

The Groundhog Mom

Did you know the mother groundhog carries her young for about 32 days? She can give birth from 2 to 6 babies. She will nurse them milk from her body. After the babies grow hair and can see, the mother will introduce them to the wild. She will encourage them to copy her behaviors so they will learn how to forage for food.

Baby Groundhogs

Did you know baby groundhogs are called pups or kits? Newborn groundhogs are born naked and blind. They are also totally helpless for about a month. Soon they will begin to make short trips outside of the burrows. They will eat grass and clover and learn how to watch out for predators.

Life of a Groundhog

Did you know in the wild, groundhogs can live up to six years-old? However, due to its many predators, it usually only lives about 2 or 3 years. In captivity, groundhogs have been know to live from 9 to 14 years-old. Groundhogs are great animals. If you ever have a chance to see one in a zoo or even in the wild, you won't be disappointed.

Yellow-bellied Marmot

Did you know this rodent is closely related to the Groundhog? It gets its name from the yellow fur on its belly. The rest of its coat is brown, with a white patch of fur between its eyes and a reddish-brown tail. It can grow to be around 11 pounds (5 kilograms). It is sometimes called, a Rock Chuck.

Hoary Marmot

Did you know this relative of the groundhog gets its name from its fur color? The word "hoary" refers to the silver-gray fur on its shoulders and upper back. The rest of its body is a drab, reddish-brown color. It is found in some parts of Canada, Alaska and the United States.

Quiz

Question 1: What other names is the groundhog called?

Answer 1: A woodchuck, a whistle-pig and a land-beaver.

Question 2: What type of body does the groundhog have?

Answer 2: Low-to-the-ground and stocky with short legs

Question 3: What does the groundhog use its sharp claws for?

Answer 3: Digging tunnels

Question 4: How long can groundhogs live in captivity?

Answer 4: 9 to 14 years-old

Question 5: What is closely related to the groundhog?

Answer 5: The Marmot

Thank you for checking out another title from Curious Kids Press! Make sure to search "Curious Kids Press" on Amazon.com for many other great books.

Made in the USA
Columbia, SC
04 February 2018